Culbone, Oare and Brendon
Remote Exmoor Parishes

Culbone, Oare and Brendon

Remote Exmoor Parishes

DENNIS CORNER

Dennis Corner.

RARE BOOKS AND BERRY
2008

This edition first published in 2008 by

Rare Books and Berry
High Street, Porlock,
Minehead, Somerset
TA24 8PU

www.rarebooksandberry.co.uk

2 4 6 8 10 9 7 5 3 1

© Dennis Corner

A CIP catalogue record for this title is
Available from the British Library

ISBN 978-0-9557119-0-9

Designed and typeset in Minion at
Alacrity, Sandford, Somerset

Printed and bound by
Biddles Ltd, King's Lynn

CONDITIONS OF SALE

Author's Acknowledgements

I WOULD LIKE to thank everybody who has helped me with this book, especially my wife for typing the manuscript, Ron Blundell, Noah and Mary Perkins for help with computing, and finally Graham Haw of Horner Mill Services for producing the map of the parishes. All the pictures are from my own collection.

Contents

CHAPTER 1	The Border Parishes	9
CHAPTER 2	Oare and Brendon	19
CHAPTER 3	Culbone	31
CHAPTER 4	How the People Lived	49
CHAPTER 5	The Second World War	55
CHAPTER 6	And Finally!	59
	Further Reading	63

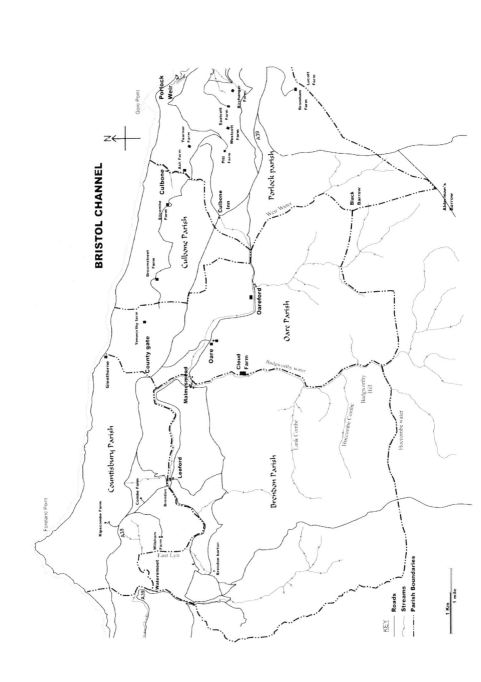

BRISTOL CHANNEL

Gore Point

Foreland Point

KEY
Roads
Streams
Parish Boundaries

1 Km
1 mile

Porlock Weir

Culbone

Culbone Parish

Slocombe Farm

Broomstreet Farm

Ash Farm

Yearnor Farm

Eastcott Farm

Westcott Farm

Pitt Farm

Blackhanger Farm

Culbone Inn

Culbone

Oareford

A39

Porlock Parish

Weir Water

Bromham Farm

Lucott Farm

Black Barrow

Alderman's Barrow

Oare Parish

Oare

Cloud Farm

Badgworthy water

Malmsmead

County gate

Yenworthy Farm

Glenthorne

Countisbury Parish

Leeford

Combe Farm

Brendon

Kipscombe Farm

A39

Wilsham Farm

East Lyn

Watersmeet

A39

Brendon barton

Brendon Parish

Lank Combe

Hoccombe Combe

Badgworthy Hill

Hoccombe water

CHAPTER 1

The Border Parishes of West Somerset and North Devon

T HIS BOOK is concerned with the Parishes of Culbone, Oare and Brendon on the border land of West Somerset and North Devon. As a long-time resident of Porlock, from where my story begins, I hope to describe this wonderful, interesting area of small villages, beautiful moorland scenery, and wooded sea cliffs and valleys. As well as some history, I will give my own memories of the places, and some of the people.

For a quick overview of this area, I will describe a journey across the high ground along the A39, between Porlock and Lynmouth. I will tell the reader my own experiences, and some of the history and legends of the area, and describe the people and how they lived.

We will start our journey in the village of Porlock. A good way to see the countryside is to take a bus, as so much more can be seen from a higher position than that in a car – although travelling by car has other advantages.

The journey takes us up the notorious Porlock Hill. It was feared by early motorists but is not as fearsome today with modern cars! The hill rises very steeply – 1 in 4 at times. At first it climbs through woodland and between fields for about a mile and a half, to a cattle grid: here the moor really begins. We are now at about 800 feet above sea level, and have reached the unfenced road where there may be sheep grazing and wandering in the road. This is a good area to see

Porlock Hill – the steepest section

Porlock Bay, with Exmoor ponies at the top of Porlock Hill

Exmoor ponies, and sometimes the wild red deer. Shortly you will reach the junction where a road goes off to the left, towards Exford. This is Whitstones Post. On the right-hand side are a couple of car parks from which, on clear days, are views over Porlock Vale to the coast of South Wales – from the Gower Peninsula down the Channel and up to Lavernock Point, near Cardiff. On our side you can see Hurlestone Point, Bossington Hill, Selworthy Beacon and North Hill, Minehead. Beyond are the Quantock Hills and the Mendip Hills, and the eastern end of Exmoor and the Brendon Hills. The highest point on Exmoor and in Somerset is Dunkery Beacon, which can also be seen from here.

Continuing on our journey, we climb up over Whitstones, named after two standing stones which can be seen on the moorland between the two roads. The stones are prehistoric. There is a legend that they were thrown from Hurlestone Point, in a contest between St Dubricius and the devil, and landed here. It is said that the devil threw a third stone which fell short, landing in the valley.

The Whitstones on Porlock Hill

The devil exclaimed, 'Poor luck!' – and that, it is said, is how Porlock got its name! In actual fact the name is of Saxon origin. And because the huge pebble ridge along the shore shut off the entrance to the land at that time, the port of Porlock was land-locked, so the harbour was developed at Porlock Weir to the western end of the bay. In recent times the sea has broken through the pebble ridge and now floods the marsh on most tides, turning it into a salt marsh.

As you now travel on, you are at about 1,400 feet above sea level, looking down on to a deep wooded valley, Worthy Combe. Pitt Farm House can be seen deep down, and further away beyond it Yearnor Farm. We shall see many isolated farms on our journey.

Shortly you reach Pitt Combe Head, where the Porlock toll road joins the A39. You have now travelled three miles. From here, on a clear day, can be seen up channel Weston-super-Mare seafront and the town of Clevedon – and with binoculars both Severn bridges.

On the left is the AA box number 137, one of the oldest in the

From Porlock Hill looking down Worthy Combe
to the sea and the South Wales Coast

country; although the second one on the site, it is a listed building. It is interesting that the AA men used to keep a water barrel regularly topped up in order that cars with radiators which had boiled up climbing Porlock Hill could, after cooling, be replenished. It was here that, on the morning following the Lynmouth flood of August 15th 1952, the first message out to the rest of the world was telephoned by a young police constable, Derek Harper. He had been on duty all night, and had lost contact with his headquarters at Barnstaple. All communications had been swept away and there was no radio contact. In the early morning he had managed, to cross the flooded river Lyn with the aid of a rope, the Lyndale bridge having been washed away. He borrowed a car from an hotelier on Countisbury Hill in order to get to Porlock to raise the alarm. Fortunately when he reached the AA box he was able to ring from there. In recognition of the wonderful work he did during all the long hours of the flood, he was awarded the George Cross.

Culbone Stables Inn, where coaching horses were changed

To the left of the AA box is a track across the moor which is an ancient ridgeway. Our road also mainly follows the coastal ridgeway to the west but, as there are many tumuli and barrows, the modern road had deviated from the original ancient way in places. The next turning to the left, Oare Post, goes down to the village of Oare, which you will read about later.

We now pass through an area of trees, some overhanging the road, which were planted many years ago. Some were found to be of little use for timber, being planted on poor rocky ground on a windswept hill. As the road descends steeply, on the left is the Culbone Stables Inn; this was where the horses were changed on the stagecoach journey from Minehead to Lynton. The last stagecoaches were replaced by charabancs in the 1920s.

Soon we pass Lillycombe House on the left, the property of the Earl of Lytton who owns much of the land we pass through. You will notice many fields and lots of sheep. Much of this land was just

Southern Wood, between Oare and Brendon

moorland until the Second World War, when for many years land was claimed from the heather moors to increase agricultural and grazing acreage, to help make the country self-supporting. This ploughing up of moorland has now been discontinued, and Exmoor still has much wild moorland, as it has for hundreds of years.

As the journey continues, there are views across the Oare valley and, further to the left, across the forest of Exmoor. 'Forest' does not mean trees – Exmoor forest has very few trees; it has the meaning of an area for hunting, formerly to preserve the King's deer, which came under strict forest laws. We shall also look down on the Oare valley, with Oare Church, the Manor House and the 'Lorna Doone' Farm, which can be reached at the next turning left. We continue to County Gate, where Somerset meets Devon. Here there is a car park; on the left is the county boundary wall which drops down over a very steep hill to the river below: this is the East Lyn.

From here you can see up through the Badgworthy valley from

Glenthorne House

Malmsmead to Cloud Farm and beyond. Opposite is Southern Wood, and the road and river running down towards the village of Brendon. The track up over the hill from the car park was once the old route to Lynmouth; the modern road now skirts the side of the hill. Beside the road can be seen the old stone gate posts and the little house, which used to be a visitor centre during the summer season.

About half a mile further on there is a layby on the left. It will be worth your while to stop here if you can. There is a footpath going away to the left and in a few minutes you can reach what I consider to be one of the best viewpoints in the area to see the Oare valley. You are on level ground, which then steeply slopes down to the valley and the river between Malmsmead and Brendon. Also, from where you have parked the car you will see, on the opposite side of the road, the entrance to the drive which descends to the lovely

Tudor-style house, Glenthorne, built in about 1830. The drive winds down the steep combe and is three miles long. The house was built by the Reverend Halliday, who owned the estate. To the left of the drive, you can see the track to Old Barrow on the brow of the hill. This was a Roman signal station early in the first century AD, manned by about eighty soldiers under a centurion, their duty being to watch over the Channel in case the Silures, the Celtic people of South Wales, tried to invade. The Romans had a port at Sea Mills, which they knew as Abona, on the Bristol Avon. The garrison was probably supplied by sea. Later another station was built on the hill between Woody Bay and Hunters Inn, further down the coast.

We now proceed towards Lynmouth, passing a few farms on the right and the first road to Brendon on the left. Some farms are known to be over five hundred years old and have descriptive names such as Wingate, Dogsworthy and Desolate. Some of the fields beside the road were created in the 1950s by ploughing up virgin moorland. After another mile we come to a very sharp bend to the left with a deep combe where there is a house which was formerly the Countisbury School and School House. We are now in the parish of Countisbury.

Brendon is in the valley on the left. We will shortly take the wider road on the left to Brendon village, but before going down to the village stop at the wide parking area at the start of the road. From here there are wonderful views of the valley of the Lyn, and in the distance Lynton.

CHAPTER 2

Oare and Brendon

MY INTEREST in these villages goes back to when, at the age of 7, I made my first visit to Oare and Brendon with two Porlock men, when they were delivering corn by lorry from Cape's the Corn Merchant in Porlock. Later I went on a Scarlet Pimpernel coach from Porlock to Lynmouth and Lynton, and then up the valley as far as Malmsmead. Even at that early age I was impressed by the journey. At some time I had a child's version of the novel *Lorna Doone* with drawings on each page of the book, which I read over and over. Later I read the full-length novel several times.

This left me with a romantic view of the area where, in later years, I walked and camped many times with the Scouts in all weathers, in Weir Wood or Malmsmead. On one occasion I remember two of us hiking from Porlock to Malmsmead during a thunder storm. It was wartime and we didn't meet anyone or any traffic. This would be difficult to accomplish today, there are so many vehicles on the roads.

The economy of the area today is mainly farming and tourism. The farms raise sheep and beef cattle, which also graze on the moorlands, where the farmers have right of grazing on the common. Crops such as oats and root crops, as well as hay, are grown and harvested, mainly to feed the farm animals.

The tourist trade rose rapidly from the middle of the nineteenth century; the publishing of *Lorna Doone* in 1869 encouraged thousands to visit the area. The main route is the A39 from Porlock to Lynmouth, which was served by stagecoach until the early 1920s, after which a regular daily bus service came into use. Today most

Robbers Bridge

travellers arrive by car. The lesser road through Oare and Brendon is quite narrow.

Oare is a small village scattered along the valley where the road runs close to Oare Water, beginning at Robbers Bridge. The road which comes off the A39 at Oare Post is known as Hookway. We can follow this to Oare Ford, where there are a farm and a few cottages, one of which was the former school. Here Oare Water is joined by another stream, Chalk Water. Further down we pass more cottages, the Rectory and Oare Church, with Oare Manor next to it. The church is one of the most visited in the West of England, due no doubt to associations with *Lorna Doone*. The Reverend John Blackmore, grandfather of the author Richard Duddridge Blackmore, was one-time rector of Oare, and it is assumed that Richard must have stayed with his grandfather and absorbed the atmosphere of Exmoor. The church is famous as the scene of the shooting of Lorna. This

Oare Ford Farm

wonderful story, which the author subtitles 'A Romance of Exmoor', brings thousands to visit the area and to see for themselves the Doone Valley, which the outlaws occupied, and Oare, where the hero John Ridd and his family lived. At one time it was said that outlaws were living at Badgeworthy; there are still remnants of ruins in the valley. The hamlet appears to have been deserted in the Middle Ages. Blackmore must have seen these ruins and set this area in his book as the Valley of the Doones.

The church, which probably dates from the fourteenth century, would have been smaller in the seventeenth century, the time of Blackmore's novel, comprising just a nave and inner chancel with a wagon roof. This must be understood when trying to reconstruct the shooting incident. The altar would have been in the inner chancel as the present chancel was not built until the nineteenth century, and the tower was rebuilt at the same time.

Oare Church

Another newer, wider road now comes down from the A39 to join the valley road at Oare Church.

Carrying on down the valley, we pass a few houses and the former Village Hall, where at one time whist drives, dances and plays were held. People attended these events from as far away as Porlock and

*Oare Church interior, made famous by R.D. Blackmore as the Church
where Carver Doone shot Lorna*

Lynmouth, as well as the surrounding farms, sometimes walking
home afterwards late at night. Later the hall was used by the Minehead and Exmoor Natural History Society for seasonal displays, and
as a starting point for their walks.

Cloud Farm, situated in Badgworthy valley, popular for riding and refreshments

View up the Oare valley from Ashton Cleeve,
with Southern Wood on the right

We now come to the 'Lorna Doone' farm, the proper name of which is Malmsmead, or 'Meadow of the Moles'. It is here that the river comes down under a high road bridge and over the ford. The river is Badgeworthy Water, pronounced 'Badgery'. It joins the Oare Water, where it becomes the East Lyn. Part of the river is the boundary between Somerset and Devon. Malmsmead is no longer a working farm. There is now a café and a shop selling souvenirs to the many tourists. There is also a National Park car park and campsite. A footpath from here can be followed up Badgeworthy Water to Cloud Farm, and on up to the Doone Valley, with a lovely walk back over Brendon Common; it will take the walker about half a day. There are many good walks in this area, and also over the rest of Exmoor. Most

The Bridge and Ford at Malmsmead

paths are 'way-marked' and looked after by the Exmoor National Park.

Leaving Malmsmead, the road follows the river for about two miles before it reaches the village of Brendon.

✦

We now come to Brendon village. It once had two mills, a blacksmith, two bakers, a post office, a village shop and a chapel. Groceries, meat and fish were delivered from Porlock and Lynmouth. Brendon still has a popular inn, The Stag Hunters.

Today it all looks very tranquil, but on August 15th 1952 it was very different. That was the night of the Lynmouth flood disaster. Properties in both Oare and Brendon suffered, some at Brendon

Bridge House at Brendon, with the former blacksmith's shop on the right

being very badly damaged. People spent a terrifying night in their houses where the water in some reached to the top of the stairs. Furniture was wrecked, as were tractors and the public telephone box. Some Scouts camping were flooded out and spent the night upstairs in a nearby house. The next day help came from the Red Cross and other organisations.

Further down the valley is the little hamlet of Rockford, which has only a few houses and the Rockford Inn. Many visitors to the villages come not only for the walking, pony riding and peace of the country-side but also to fish the river Lyn for brown trout and salmon, or to attend the local hunts – the Devon and Somerset Staghounds and the Exmoor Foxhounds. The Foxhounds were at one time kennelled at Oare Manor.

Brendon: the village street

These days there is an annual pony sale when ponies are brought off the moor to be sold, and there is the annual Brendon Show in August.

Brendon Church is about 700 feet above sea level, and approximately one mile west of the village, situated at the top of a 1 in 4 hill. It is dedicated to St Brendan, born in Tralee, County Kerry in AD 484, a much-travelled navigator who sailed in the North Atlantic. The church, built in 1738, replaced the church at Cheriton, the hamlet on the other side of Farley Water, three miles from the village of Brendon. Some of the old stone was used, as well as other items such as the Norman font and a slate sundial of 1707, which can be seen over the front porch.

Just beyond the church is the former village school. It is amazing at the present time to think that about thirty children used to attend Brendon School, with others from the top end of the village attending the school in the neighbouring parish of Countisbury. Both

Brendon Church

closed after the Second World War. The children would walk to and from school as there were no buses or cars. One can imagine the difficulties some children must have had, walking across fields and moorland in bad Exmoor weather, probably getting wet through by the time they arrived at school, and later having to cope with the journey home.

Another school situated at Oare Ford, which closed in 1932, only had about nine pupils towards the end, and some of them walked from Broomstreet in Culbone parish.

CHAPTER 3

Culbone

T HE BEST WAY to visit Culbone – in fact the only way for most
people – is to walk! The only vehicular access is for residents
and farmers. But it must be emphasised that the walk is only
for those who are fit. It is now more strenuous than ever as landslips
have necessitated the cutting of steps up to a higher track. I suggest
that visitors should park at Porlock Weir car park; there is a signpost
showing the route. The right-of-way signs are on the left wall of the
Anchor Hotel and the path goes up behind the hotel. There is another
path which goes up some steps just beyond the industrial units, past
the Boatshed, a maritime museum which is well worth visiting and
which gives much information of the past life of this little fishing
community.

Both paths lead into a meadow, and the footpath continues for
about half a mile through three meadows until it joins the top road
above the village. You are now at Worthy, where there are the remains
of a former farm, and just beyond is a fine house called Worthy
Manor, some parts of which go back to the thirteenth century. In the
early part of the twentieth century the architect C.F. Annesley Voisey
improved this house, and others in the area including Ashley Combe;
he also designed the new reredos in Culbone Church in 1928. Shortly
you will arrive at the gatehouse of the Worthy toll road. Ahead you
will see the sign to Culbone: 'Public Path'.

You will still be in Porlock Parish until you reach the stream at
Culbone Church. Culbone as a civil parish was united with Oare in
1933. The owner of much of the land was the Earl of Lovelace, whose

Porlock Weir

Worthy Manor, near Porlock Weir

estate was at Ashley Combe. The first Lord Lovelace married Ada, daughter of the poet Lord Byron. It was Lord Lovelace who created the house, now demolished, at Ashley Combe, enlarging the existing house in about 1839, creating tunnels and gardens – several tunnels led to the house and grounds. The house was built in the Italianate style: he had visited Northern Italy many times and loved to climb the Alps, having previously practised on the local sea cliffs. One of the visitors to the house was Charles Babbage, the inventor of the first computer. He collaborated with Lady Lovelace, who was a brilliant mathematician – she was probably the world's first computer programmer! That is why the computer centre in Porlock is named the Lovelace Centre.

The present Toll House with the archway was the gatehouse to the mansion and the nearby stables and carriage house – these have been converted into dwellings which can be seen from the start of the

Ashley Combe House, demolished in the 1960s

Ashley Combe Gatehouse: the tollgate and entrance to Culbone path

public path. This path takes you through a tunnel and shortly there is a building on your left. This was at the end of what was known as the Philosopher's Walk. From here Lord and Lady Lovelace and their guests could look out at the sea – the view is now obscured by tall trees. Also from here there was a winding pathway down the cliffs to Rockford Cottage, believed to have been a boathouse and bathing place for Lady Lovelace. It has long been a ruin. At one time the boatmen of Porlock Weir advertised trips on fine summer days which took visitors around the bay and to view the 'Smugglers' Cottage', which was Rockford Cottage. Perhaps it could have been used by smugglers at some time!

It was in 1682 that His Majesty's Surveyor General of Customs visited the county and wrote a long, horrified report on the illegal traffic which sustained all the small ports, often with the connivance of local Justices of the Peace. He reported:

I went to visit Porlock, which is about four miles from Minehead, where there is a deep bay and a good harbour for small vessels, to which place there are several that belong, which trade overseas. The [preventive] officer; Richard Davis, is an active young fellow, hath hitherto been paid £5 per ann, by incidents; he very well deserves £10 and be stablished, it being a place of trade and great quantities of herrings are taken and cured, which begets a great concourse of people and small craft, that may be of dangerous consequence to the crown unless well guarded.

Over the centuries smuggling flourished around our coast and was prevalent in Cornwall, Devon and Somerset. Lynmouth and Porlock were no exception. In 1886 a ship named the *Mabel* went down off Nash Point after colliding with the schooner *Harkaway*. The *Mabel*, a British ship, carried a cargo of sugar, rum and coconuts, and for days after her wrecking the tide was casting up huge barrels of rum on this side of the Channel. The men of Porlock Weir needed no bidding to be in attendance. Years later someone told the *West Somerset Free Press* how he watched the barrels, each six or seven feet high, rolling in with the tide. The young boys' quest was for the coconuts which had been used to keep the barrels in position in the ship's hold. But the adults were more interested in the bigger and

Landslide at Rockford Cottage

stronger libation. Along the coast, from the Weir to Culbone, men were tapping the barrels and filling smaller kegs from them. Some hid their kegs in Culbone woods and, although the Customs men came on the scene as quickly as possible to perform a legitimate pick-up, they knew they were many barrels down. News of the rum reached the 'inlanders', and one man came all the way from Wootton Courtenay with a cart filled with straw in which he could hide a cask. Rum and coconuts also came ashore all along the coast from Porlock Weir to Helwell Bay at Watchet, but the main concentration had been at Porlock, where the initiative in accepting the sea's gifts was second to none!

I remember, when I was young, huge barrels of wine being washed up on Porlock beach. They were retrieved by Customs officers, impounded and sealed. Unfortunately the wine had been spoiled by sea water, so the barrels were all drained out.

Many times I have visited Rockford Cottage and Ashley Combe. Unfortunately the land often slides away on this unstable cliffside so that, not only has the path gone, but it won't be long before the cottage itself disappears. As late as the 1950s the public path to Culbone was at a much lower level. As boys we used to throw stones from the path into the sea. The mail van, as well as residents and occasionally traders, once used the higher path; I once drove a van to Culbone myself. The lower path was very level and smooth and I recall that another boy and I rode our bikes from Culbone to Ashley Combe Lodge in three minutes!

The woods through to Culbone and beyond are lovely. They have been managed for timber over the years. There used to be a sawmill in Worthy Combe driven by water power. At one time there were over twenty men employed on the forestry work, and there were lots of red squirrels to be seen, as well as red deer, foxes and badgers. Back in 1800s there were also pine martens and a herd of feral goats, such as there are in the Valley of Rocks at Lynton. The goats caused so much destruction that the local farmers organised a shoot. They drove them up through a valley, and guns posted on either side shot them. The head of the huge billy was mounted, and was given years

Culbone: what was once the potter's house

later to the Porlock Branch of TocH by Alec Corruthers Gould, the
local artist. It hung for several years in their meeting room in Parson
Street, but was attacked by insects and had to be taken down and
burned. The reason for goats living in Culbone Woods was that two
ladies living at Yenworthy wanted goats' milk, and unfortunately the
animals escaped.

For many years, from 1919 to 1957, the post was delivered by Frank
Glanville of Porlock. At first he walked in all weathers to Culbone
and several of the hill farms, a round trip of twenty miles. Later he
used a motorbike and side car. Since then a van has been used by the
postmen, but they can no longer deliver to Culbone as the track is
closed from Worthy Combe. Prior to this post had to be collected

Silcombe Farm, above Culbone

from Porlock or Porlock Weir; at present it is left for collection at
Ashley Combe Lodge.

I can recall many walks to Culbone. It is a very peaceful valley,
almost enclosed by steep wooded hillsides; it is said that the sun only
shines on it for nine months of the year.

Culbone is a small parish which has only two cottages remaining
near the church, but there are several farms and scattered cottages
within the parish. The surrounding farms of Silcombe, Parsonage,
Broomstreet, Ash, Yearnor and Pitt have all been supporters of
Culbone Church. The Rector, who resided at Oare for many years, is
taken down from Silcombe in a Land Rover. Culbone is famous for
having the smallest complete parish church in England. Situated in

Culbone Church, the smallest complete parish church in England

Culbone Church interior

*Culbone Church window, hewn from one piece of stone,
with a carved animal face*

a steep combe 400 feet above sea level, it consists of a chancel and nave with a south porch, and is said to seat 33 people uncomfortably. It has been altered frequently during its long history. It has been suggested that lepers also lived and worked in the woods. This is probably true. Stories tend to be handed down for generations, and the disease was prevalent in Britain during the Middle Ages. There is a small window on the north side of Culbone Church to allow those outside to view the service.

Of the early history of Culbone little is known. The ancient name was Kitnor, said to be from the Anglo-Saxon. The name Culbone probably indicated a Celtic religious site, being a corruption of Kil Bean, or Church of St Beuno. St Beuno was a Welsh saint in Powis in the sixth century. Many Celtic saints' names are common in dedication, for example St Dubricius at Porlock, St Decuman at Watchet and St Brendan, who is remembered at Brendon.

Parsonage Farm, near Culbone

It is well known that the poets Samuel Taylor Coleridge and William Wordsworth, and Wordsworth's sister Dorothy, walked a number of times through this area to Porlock, admiring the scenery, and visited the 'Valley of the Stones', as they used to call the Valley of Rocks at Lynton. This was during the few years that they resided at Nether Stowey. In the autumn of 1797 Coleridge, on his way back from Lynton and walking alone, stayed overnight at a lonely farmhouse which years later he described as being about half a mile from Culbone Church. No one is certain which farm this was. It was here that he took two grains of opium, to which he had become addicted, and fell into a reverie. On waking, he began to write about his vision in the poem 'Kubla Khan'. His train of inspiration was apparently interrupted by a caller, after which he could remember nothing more about his dream. That 'Person from Porlock' has been blamed ever since for his not completing one of his greatest poems.

In 1800 the Reverend Richard Warner of Bath wrote *A Walk Through Some of the Western Counties of England* – these days a very rare book – in which he describes his visit to West Somerset. His writing is very descriptive of that age. He walked from Porlock to the moorland above Culbone with his guide, a Porlock shoemaker who knew the area well. Coming to a dilapidated cottage and seeing a few cows, he called and asked if they could have a glass of milk. The old lady said no: they could get milk at Silcombe Farm a bit further on, but not at the Parsonage. The Reverend Warner found it hard to believe that the old cottage had once been the Parsonage, but his guide assured him that previously it had been much better. After calling at Silcombe, they went down by a very declivitous track to Culbone, where they found the little church, two dilapidated cottages and the ruins of a few others. Here he met an old blacksmith who told him that he remembered the time, fifty odd years before, when he came to the 'Culbone Revel' held in the churchyard. This, I imagine, was a 'Church Ale' – in those days these were held to raise money for the upkeep of churches. Over three hundred people had been there! The blacksmith told the Reverend Warner that, although he had had too much to drink, he decided to have a go at skittles (nine pins) in order to win the prize. The result was that he lost his golden half guinea, which was about all he had. Feeling upset, he went to the stream to swill off his face and head, realising that the drink had upset his aim. Refreshed, the effect of the drink wearing off, he had more goes at the skittles and was able to win back his money. He then vowed never to gamble again!

Also in the book is a sketch of the church as it then was. John Collinson, writing in 1791, describes the church as covered with Cornish tiles. These were large hand-cut slabs similar to those seen on the Old Post Office at Tintagel. The church was restored in about 1810, and the spire was erected.

The Reverend H.J. Marshall, a former Rector, describes an event at Culbone Church:

The next incident also concerned a Parish Clerk, one of those men of out-standing character who played so noteworthy a part in the Parish life of bygone days. The scene was Culbone Church, where visitors were few and far between, and created considerable interest among the small congregation who worshipped there. One Sunday there were two visitors who had walked from Porlock Weir, and as it was full summer they were dressed in white. All went well until the Rector gave out as his text: 'Who are these arrayed in white robes and whence come they?' He was an impressive preacher, and kept repeating his text, his eyes fixed on the unfortunate visitors. At last, Nat Cook, the parish Clerk, could stand the strain no longer and answered back: 'I don't exactly know who they be, but I believe they're stoppin' at the Anchor.'

After the Second World War on the Ashley Combe Estate, which included Culbone Woods, there was much timber felling, the Earl of Lytton employing over twenty men on the operations. Various types of trees were felled. The straight timbers from firs and larch were used as pit props; other timber such as oak and ash was sawn up on a tractor-driven circular saw and served as logs for domestic use. One boat-load was sent to Bristol on a return journey after bringing coal to Porlock Weir. Other timber was sawn at Ashley Combe Saw Mill and used to make gates and hurdles; gate posts were stood in a heated tank of creosote to preserve the wood. Also, Alfie and Billy Cook of

Ash Farm

West Porlock were allowed to cut ferns, which were sent by rail to London, where they were used in Covent Garden to display the fish for sale.

There are stories of charcoal burners living in Culbone Woods years ago. Whether they lived in the woods at all times or came there from the surrounding area is not known. Charcoal burning is a very slow process, taking several days, as the fire must not be allowed to flare; earth is shovelled on to exclude the air. Men needed to be in attendance day and night during a burning, so they built huts to sleep in. Charcoal pits, where the fires were made, are still to be found in the woods. The three Priscott boys whose parents once farmed at Ash knew where these pits were as they used to comb the wood collecting stags' horns, of which they had many pairs. They, also in their exploration, found a number of flint arrowheads from the distant

The Culbone kist, showing coffin and skull

days of the hunter gatherers. Charcoal was exported with tan bark from the beach at Embelle Wood to South Wales.

Above Culbone the modern A39 for the most part follows the south side the ancient ridgeway. The map shows many tumuli along the route. It was in 1897 that a road worker called Moore, who was digging out stone from the quarry beyond the entrance of Broomstreet Farm, struck into a 'kist' – more correctly a 'kistvane' – containing a stone coffin, with a beaker beside what the only description of this event called a 'grinning skeleton'. How it could be grinning after some three thousand years I know not. When the stage coach came by and the coachman stopped to look, he saw the beaker and took it away! But the authorities got it back, and it can be seen with the kist and skeleton in Taunton Museum. The body was that of one of the 'beaker folk', who came from Europe and settled here many

The Culbone Stone

years BC. They were noted for burying their dead with a beaker, usually with a highly decorated rim. Perhaps they believed they would need a drink on their way to another world.

Opposite Culbone Stables Inn the road leads down to Worthy Combe, and the track to the hill farms. After crossing the cattle grid there is a sign where you can follow a footpath a short distance to the Culbone Stone. This is a standing stone about 2 foot 6 inches high with a wheeled cross carved into it in a style thought to be sixth century. One arm of the cross comes outside the wheel and is believed to be a pointer towards Culbone Church. In early times, unlike today, there were of course few signs; early people would simply follow landmarks.

Also, there is a stone row going from West to East between two barrows. It is on private land, which is fenced off, but I was given permission some years ago to go in to find the stones. I found eleven, though others previously recorded as many as twenty. Over the years some may have been lost due to the timber operations. I have wondered if the ancient people were sun worshippers because, if they had walked along that row in the early morning, they would have seen the sun rising over Hurlestone. Even today there are those who climb hills on Easter morning to see the sun rise, celebrating the resurrection of Christ, and others who visit Stonehenge to see the sun rise on midsummer day.

CHAPTER 4

How the People Lived

FROM EARLY times people lived in the parishes, as witnessed by the barrows, standing stones and hut circles that are to be found on the moors. There was also a Roman fortlet at Old Barrow overlooking the sea. There were always deer and wild ponies to be found, and the parishes bounded what later became the Royal Forest of Exmoor.

In the early Norman period the three parishes were part of the forest and the inhabitants came under the very strict forest law. However, together with others from around Exmoor and beyond, they pastured their sheep and cattle on the forest during the summer. Of course the Wardens of the forest had to be paid for this privilege.

After disafforestation in the reign of King John, the farmers had right of common over the commons of the parish. This meant that they had certain privileges: as well as being allowed to pasture their animals, they could also cut ferns for their animals' bedding, cut turf (peat) and collect wood for the fires in their homes. Right up to the present time certain parishioners exercise these rights. Farming was mainly pasture, with stock and hay, but some corn was grown, such as oats and rye, and root crops for the cattle.

During the Middle Ages the Lords of the Manor were the owners of each particular manor. In the middle of the tenth century land was given to the Brethren Knights of the order of St John of Jerusalem. This was Baggeworth or Badgeworthy, known today as 'Badgery'. Here there was a small settlement of fourteen houses and a chapel,

Combe Farm, Brendon, a typical Exmoor farm

which mainly fell into ruin in the fourteenth and fifteenth centuries. The Manor later passed into the hands of the Harrington family, who also owned Porlock. The fourth Baron Harrington and his wife are depicted in the wonderful monument in Porlock Church. After her husband's death Lady Harrington often visited both Porlock and Brendon.

Here is some of the information taken from her Bailiff Roger Trypa's rolls, dated Michaelmas 1422 to Michaelmas 1423. There were 38 tenants of the Manor of Brendon. The annual rent from the village of Badgeworthy was 12 shillings. The Lady, now a widow, also received agisment, i.e. payment for cattle pastured on her moorland, and for the sale of pasturage. She received payments for the sale of one ox, six cows, three heifers and three steers. There were also problems at that time with foot-and-mouth disease.

Payments of 2s 4d were made to the Forest of Exmoor for the keep of Lady Harrington's beasts in the summer time. The cost of four thousand stone tiles for her house was 4s 8d. Bread and beer bought

Everyone turned out on a hunting day

for the men who carried the tiles was 4d. One thousand lathe nails cost 15d.

Four men hired to drive divers of the Lady's beasts from Brendon to Porlock earned 8d. One man hired to drive the Lady's 114 geese from Brendon to Porlock received 4d. The driving of these animals to Porlock was probably for the market or fair day. Men were also paid to clean ditches and repair fences, and to mow, spread, gather, cock and carry the hay. Payments were also made to divers men hired to cleanse the house at Brendon against the coming of the Lady.

We also learn from the document that the Lady sold a heifer on occasions and gave the money towards the building of a Weir at West Porlock. This is probably the first mention of Porlock Weir.

We can see from all this how different life was at that time, when the fastest form of transport was the horse. It didn't change a great deal until improved roads made the area more accessible.

Early tourists usually arrived by stagecoach or horse bus, and later by charabanc or motor car. The nearest railway stations were at

Stage Coach at the Blue Ball, Countisbury

Taunton (opened in 1842), Barnstaple (1854) and Minehead (1874). A narrow gauge line was opened between Barnstaple and Lynton in 1898, and served until its closure in 1935. It would have been a great event to go each autumn to Barnstaple to visit the famous Barnstaple Fair.

The farms, though, continued in the same old ways into the twentieth century, being worked with horses and oxen. They didn't improve a great deal until the coming of tractors, and the incentive to plough up moorland during the Second World War. This of course meant that more stock could be kept on the fields than had previously been kept on moorland. The farmers' wives mainly stayed at home to look after their children, perhaps also taking in paying guests. They would keep a few milking cows so that they could make cream, butter and cheese.

Lizzie Cook and her husband Tom lived in the cottage next to Culbone Church for years. Lizzie came up from Cornwall on a bicycle in 1913 to visit her relatives; she married her cousin Tom and never returned to Cornwall! She died in 1981. While at Culbone she looked after the church for many years and served teas for her many visitors – not only from this country but also from many parts of the world. Many would send her postcards; her room used to be full of them. Often she received large parties of walkers, all pleased to enjoy her tea and scones, or bread with cream and jam. Her water was boiled in a kettle on the kitchen range and she kept a brick in the oven to use, wrapped in flannel, as a bed-warmer. She often visited Porlock or Porlock Weir for social events and had no fear of walking home late at night through Culbone Woods, even during the autumn rutt of the stags. 'They won't hurt me,' she said, 'I'm not afraid. I just speak and they know who I am.'

Tom was a groom. At one time he worked at Porlockford with the horses. I remember he drove a large Ford V8 Pilot and offered some of us young lads a ride back from Culbone along the top woodland track to Ashley Combe. He drove like a fiend, the vehicle swaying from side to side and the lads in the back holding on for dear life.

In the 1950s to '70s the world-renowned potter Waistel-Cooper had a pottery at Culbone. He and his wife Joan lived in the cottage up from the church. Much of his fine work can still be seen in the district. Formerly in Iceland, he moved to Porlock where he set up a pottery in Bossington Lane before coming to Culbone. His kiln was fired by Calor gas, and much of the clay he used was local, from near Broomstreet Farm.

Joan wrote a booklet, *Culbone: A Spiritual History* – a strange work which goes back thousands of years and continues through to recent times. She tells of prisoners of war from India being in Culbone, and lepers and charcoal burners being outlawed. As far as I know there is no documentation to support this. When questioned, she answered that it had been 'revealed' to her. I cannot say that it is not true. Perhaps she had a spiritual knowledge that most of us do not have. She was a fine lady, whom I knew; a lay reader who also played the organ for services in the church. When Joan died, her husband left Culbone and moved to Penzance.

Today the villages are still remote and quiet places for most of the year, although they can occasionally be busy in the summer months. The main change in modern times has been that fewer people now work the land as more machinery is bought for use on the farms. Many houses are occupied by retired people; there are fewer young families than there were in the past. People are more mobile now and not confined to a close, secluded life in which they seldom leave the area.

CHAPTER 5

The Second World War

IN 1940 the Local Defence Volunteers (LDV), later renamed the
Home Guard, was formed. One of the duties of members, at
the little bungalow at Yearnor Moor Lodge, opposite Culbone
Stables Inn, was to take turns to patrol and watch for parachutists. It
was believed that the Germans might try to invade in the South West,
dropping troops on Exmoor or the Blackdown Hill.

Laurie Perkins was one of the young men involved; he was later
called up to the regular Army and served in India. He says that the
Home Guard issued him with a rifle but no ammunition. He questioned what he might do with the rifle: 'Hit them over the head with
it?' Later Bill Huish came up from Porlock on his motorbike to tell
them that two extra men would be coming as there was a report that
Germans had been seen landing on the beach. At Oare and Brendon
the Home Guard Unit were mounted on Exmoor ponies.

In the early days of the war there was a searchlight battery
stationed near Culbone Stables. The concrete bases of their huts can
still be seen beyond the fence at the side of the road. Further down
towards Yearnor, at Stent hill, were a number of buildings which the
RAF used as a radar station. The men who worked there were lodged
at several farms in the area, and were sworn to secrecy. They could
not even tell their wives about the work they were doing. Three of
the huts are still standing and can be seen on the skyline. They are
now used as farm buildings.

Those were desperate times, in 1940. A Greek cargo ship ran ashore
at Embelle beach, and remained there for several days. Eventually, on

the next high tide and with the help of a tug, she was refloated. The ship had chickens and goats on board, presumably to supply fresh eggs and milk.

Ewart Perkins was an Auxiliary Coastguard. One of his duties was to walk the beach from Porlock Weir to Glenthorne every day, one way along the beach, the other through the woods, depending on the tide. One lovely day he arrived at Glenthorne beach to find a elderly lady sitting there reading. He was sorry, he told her, but he would have to ask her to leave the beach. She replied that she had no intention of leaving: it was a private beach. Mr Perkins continued, 'I think you had better move quickly – you are leaning against a mine!'

It was a huge mine that had been washed up on the shore. The lady rushed quickly up to the house and he soon followed in order to ask if he might phone his headquarters. Arriving at the house he saw the inhabitants were about to leave by car. However, he managed to phone and later a Royal Navy bomb disposal unit arrived. They took out the bulk of explosive, leaving only about 20 per cent, which they detonated on the beach. Even then the explosion was such that it broke several windowpanes in the house.

Many mines were laid around the coast. Some German ones were dropped by aircraft, some British ones were anchored in minefields. We also know that many ships were sunk in the Bristol Channel, either by mines or by U-boat torpedoes.

In January 1940 the winter was terrible, with much snow and freezing temperatures. The rivers of Exmoor were frozen solid. Porlock Marsh froze and many people went down to slide on the ice across the marsh. One day a large pall of smoke was seen out to the west. Many of us immediately made our way to the Porlock Weir road: from the school railings we could see that a ship was on fire. Black smoke was rising several thousand feet in the air, and flames hundreds of feet up. The ship was an oil tanker, the *Inverdargo*, built in 1938. Sailing from Trinidad to Avonmouth, carrying 12,554 tonnes of highly inflammable aviation spirit, she was struck by a torpedo from a German U-boat, U33, under the command of Hans Wilhelm Dreski. The tanker's crew of 45 were all lost. The Lynmouth boats

Shepherd's hut, probably built of stones from the ruins of
Badgworthy, demolished during the Second World War

went out and found the vessel white hot. No one could have survived.
The remains finally sank off Glenthorne, just to the Porlock side of
the Foreland Point. We now know that U-boats in the Bristol Channel often landed men in dinghies at night along the remote coast so
that they could get fresh water from the streams.

   In 1940 the Army arrived in the area. Companies of Royal Engin-
eers were billeted in Porlock and Lynton. Most of Exmoor became a
training area for both gas warfare and heavy guns and mortars. Red
flags were flown during firing days and no one was allowed on the
moors. The shepherds had to clear the moors of all stock and drive
the animals down to the farms. Some farms, such as Larkbarrow and
Tom's Hill had to be evacuated. Later American troops followed the
British and camped on the moors. Heavy guns were fired from as far
away as Fyldon Ridge near North Molton. Larkbarrow and Tom's Hill
were destroyed. The thousands of shells, many unexploded, that
littered the moors had to be cleared after the war.

During the Second World War Ashley Combe House was leased to Dr Barnardo's Homes as a children's nursery, it being unsafe for children to remain in London because of the bombing. However, on June 11th 1943 a Halifax bomber coming in from the sea in dense fog nearly crashed into the house. It took the tops off the trees over a wide area and caught fire. The scars on the trees could be seen for several years. Four airmen were killed and two injured, one of them badly burned. Men working in the woods went to their aid.

About this time the estate passed into the ownership of the Earl of Lytton. The hill farms on the estate, except for Lillycombe, had been sold to the tenant farmers. The Earl's son, the present Earl, now owns the estate.

The teenage lads of the village had a great time during the war years visiting the nurses at Ashley Combe House when they were off duty. The matron and her deputy were very good and held the occasional party, inviting the village lads. There would be a supper and perhaps some dancing, or a fancy dress party. On one occasion there was a fund-raising party for Dr Barnardo's, with stalls and competitions on the lawn.

Some of the girls also came to Porlock for Youth Club social evenings, and on Sundays to the churches. After the war Ashley Combe House was for a few years a country club, but this closed and the house was demolished in about 1960.

CHAPTER 6

And Finally!

B EYOND CULBONE Church there are paths which the walker can take, but due to landslips the South West Coast Path now takes a higher route to Glenthorne, and on to Countisbury and Lynmouth. It is possible to get down to Embelle Wood beach (pronounced 'Emmelle' by locals). It was here that limestone and coal were imported, and charcoal and tan bark exported. A lime kiln can be seen on the shore, and there is also one at Glenthorne. I can remember a boat house, with a winch and hawser for pulling a boat up over the pebbles. This beach seems to attract loose timber and debris from the sea.

One of the coastal farmers was John Red, who farmed at Broomstreet and also owned and traded with sailing ketches in the Channel. There was a winding track down to Embelle Wood beach, wide enough to take a horse and butt from Broomstreet, and to haul up lime, coal or driftwood – some of which was very good timber from wreckage, and of course useful on the farm.

Also at Embelle Wood someone made a small garden near the shore where potatoes were grown. Unfortunately some Welsh people came across one day, dug them up and took them back to Wales. This was during the years of depression when things were desperate, particularly in Wales, where there was much unemployment and poverty.

With a group of teenagers, I once walked from Porlock Weir to Glenthorne and decided to return along the beach, a distance of about five miles. This was the first time I saw Rockford Cottage,

From Gore Point, showing the woods sweeping down to the shore

which then had a wooden gate across the entrance. A little further on
the Worthy Stream discharges on to the beach. There is a lime kiln
amongst the bushes which was used when Ashley Combe House was
being built.

In the summer people often take the Lynmouth bus to Pittcombe
Head, Culbone Stables Inn or even County Gate and follow one of
the footpaths back to Porlock or down to Culbone via the hill farms
to Porlock Weir, perhaps getting a bus back to Porlock or Minehead.
One afternoon two elderly ladies I knew decided to take the bus out
and then walk down the footpath to Glenthorne via the arboretum.
After they had had a rest and it was time to catch the return bus, they
couldn't face the steep climb back up to the road – it was a very hot
day, and they had a small elderly dog with them – so they decided
to walk back along the beach. However, it is a long hard walk over
pebbles, and huge boulders and rocks in places, and the tide was

From Bossington Hill, looking over Porlock Bay to Lynmouth foreland

coming in. This eventually cut them off and they had to climb up on to the cliffs and wait for the tide to turn. They reached Porlock Weir in the dark, then had to walk to Porlock as it was too late for a bus. The poor little dog was so tired it had to be carried the rest of the way. They reached Porlock about midnight. This illustrates the danger of walking on the foreshore if you do not know the times and height of the tide. Had the coastguard station at Hurlestone Point still been operational, the coastguard would have seen those ladies on the beach and alerted a rescue team.

Just beyond Porlock Weir is Gore Point. *Gore* is an old English word for a triangular piece of land, although some people think the name derives from the days of the attack by the Danes when so much blood was shed. Here there are still several fishing weirs which can be seen at low tide. Used in the district as fish traps since medieval times, they are ponds made with large boulders, in the shape of an

'L' or 'V', with the point at the seaward end. The outlet would be blocked so that fish were trapped in them at high tide. The fishermen would then put a net or basket at the outlet, remove the large stones and let the water out, catching the fish in the net or basket. This method of fishing, still being used in recent times along the coast, was easier in winter time than going out in a boat and facing the perils of the sea. Old people of Porlock Weir used to say that the Monks of Cleeve Abbey used to use these fishing weirs. This story has been passed down for generations, so there may be truth in it. Abbeys had control of fish weirs in the Middle Ages. However it does seem a long way to come; there were nearer places such as Blue Anchor and Dunster beach.

Another method of fishing was to hang nets on stakes at the Gore. One day so many sprats were caught the fishermen had to call for help from Noah Pollard. Noah was a very strong man. His reaction was, 'They never catch more sprats than I can carry.' But when he arrived he was amazed at the number of fish. There were so many they had to get a horse and cart to carry them to Porlock Weir.

A Porlock lady once told me about her mother who was born at Porlock Weir, where her grandparents lived at Lane Head. Her grandfather was one of the local fishermen. Her mother and grandmother would regularly take fish to the hill farms, and in exchange would bring back eggs, cream and butter – a fine example of bartering as late as early twentieth century.

✷

I hope that readers of this book will be able to pay a visit to the area, preferably for a few days, and have the pleasure of discovering more about this beautiful and interesting place – the parishes of Brendon, Oare and Culbone – as well as the rest of Exmoor.

Further Reading

ALLEN, N.V. *Churches and Chapels of Exmoor.* The Exmoor Press, 1971.

ALEXANDER, Caroline. *The Way to Xanadu.* Alfred A. Knopf, New York, 1993.

BLACKMORE, R.D. *Lorna Doone.* 1869.

BOUQUET, Michael. *No Gallant Ship.* Hollis & Carter, 1959.

BURTON, S.H. *The Lorna Doone Trail.* Exmoor Press, 1975.

COLLINSON, John. *The History of Somerset.* 1701.

COLLINSON-MORLEY, Kathleen. *A Short History of West Porlock, Porlock Weir and Culbone.* Cox & Sons, 1930.

COOPER, Joan. *Culbone: A Spiritual History.* Georgian, 1977.

CHADWYCK HEALEY, Sir C.H. *History of Part of West Somerset.* Sotheran, 1901.

CORNER, Dennis. *Porlock in Those Days.* Exmoor Press, 1992.

— *The Book of Porlock.* Halsgrove, 1999/2002.

EARDLEY-WILMOT, Hazel. *Yesterday's Exmoor.* Exmoor Books, 1990.

EXMOOR NATIONAL PARK. *A Doone Country Walk.* 1993.

GAMLIN, John. *Survey of Culbone.* Unpublished. Aavailable in Porlock Library.

GREGORY, R.J. 'Mother's Uncle John', *Exmoor Review* No.3, p.53.

HALLIDAY, Ursula. *Glenthorne, A Most Romantic Place.* Exmoor Books, 1995.

HURLEY, Jack. *Exmoor in Wartime 1939-45.* Exmoor Press, 1978/1990.

LOWES, John Livingstone. *The Road to Xanadu.* 1927.

MACDERMOT, E.T. *The Forest of Exmoor.* Barnicott & Pearce, 1944.

MARSHALL, H.J. *Exmoor, Sporting and Otherwise.* Eyre & Spottiswoode, 1948.

MOLD, E.T. 'The Stone Row on Culbone Hill', *Exmoor Review* No.24. p.67.

ORWIN, C.S. & SELLICK, R.J. *The Reclamation of Exmoor Forest.* David & Charles, 1970.

PAGE, John Lloyd Warden. *An Exploration of Exmoor and the Hill Country of West Somerset.* 1890.

PORTER, H.M. *The Celtic Church in Somerset* (with a chapter on North Devon). Morgan Books, 1971.

RILEY, Hazel & WILSON NORTH, Robert. *The Field Archaeology of Exmoor.* English Heritage, 2001.

SMITH, Graham. *Shipwrecks of the Bristol Channel.* Countryside Books, Newbury, Berks, 1991.

— *Smuggling in the Bristol Channel 1700-1850.* 1989

TRAVIS, John. *Smuggling on the Exmoor Coast 1680-1850.* The Exmoor Society, 2001.

WARNER, Rev. Richard. *A Walk Through Some of the Western Counties of England.* Bath, 1800.

Files on the Local Parishes. Available to read only in Porlock Library.

Guides to Churches of Culbone, Oare and Brendon. Available in the churches.